This book, as well as my daily existence & all my money, are (were) dedicated to the mucho-groovy women in my life who make (made) each day worth getting up off the floor for: The Fantabulous Duo ~ Kaitlin & Killian, and my erstwhile wife, Kalin.

Thanks also to Mom & Dad & the Soviet Union for not blowing me away despite numerous threats, both expressed & implied. And VERY SPECIAL THANKS to all the far-out dudes & chicks who flew me, drove me, fed me, diapered me, and put me up for the night during my travels last year & this.

Available at booksellers everywhere in February of 1997 will be *Bizarro Among the Savages*, a humorous and beguiling account of much of Dan Piraro's wretched life, including the year he spent traveling across America and staying in the homes of his readers. It is *essential* reading for anyone wanting to claim they have read it and not get caught lying. As evidenced in the following excerpt, Piraro gives a lively and engaging account of his experiences on the road as he haphazardly puts his life in the hands of strangers and lives to tell about it:

To describe Ken as reserved would be like describing Hitler as cranky. No matter what either of us said, his facial expression never altered one molecule from a wide-eyed, stiff-jawed intensity that reminded me of a person sitting on a plane with a bomb hidden in their briefcase.

Our conversation was relatively bland and tense, until Ken said something that made it suddenly much less bland and a lot more tense.

"I have a confession to make," he said evenly, staring a hole straight through my head and into the cosmos as he had been since I met him. "I've never really seen your cartoons. In fact, when I invited you to stay, I didn't even know who you were. I just saw the letter you sent out on a guy's computer at work. I've never even seen your work, I just thought it might be interesting to invite you and see what happened." He waited for my response like Anthony Perkins waited for Janet Lee to get into the shower.

Not wanting to show my growing sense of alarm, I bluffed casually, "Interesting. So you've never even seen my cartoons?" I smiled as though I couldn't have cared less, but inside, my mind was running out all the possible scenarios.

"I was actually pretty surprised when you called and said you were coming," Ken went on, with a slightly malevolent smile. "It was weird at the bookstore watching people make a big fuss over you, because to me, you were just another random guy."

*Just another random victim, you mean.*

I weighed my options: I could stick it out, hope that he was just kidding, and take my chances; or I could run screaming out of the cafe and down the street, hoping to retrieve my luggage later, with a police escort . . . .

FASCINATING JUDICIAL TRIVIA —

— IT IS ILLEGAL IN 23 STATES TO CONFUSE A BABY WITH A BOAT DURING A CHRISTENING CEREMONY.

....AND REMEMBER: IF YOU SEE A WOLF, IGNORE IT; IT PROBABLY WON'T BOTHER YOU. BUT IF YOU SEE A MAN, SPRAY HIM WITH MACE AND RUN LIKE CRAZY!

FIRST ANNUAL GUY-CRAWLING-THROUGH-A-DESERT CARTOON CONVENTION

...THE MINUTES FROM THE LAST MEETING HAVE BEEN READ AND SUBMITTED. ALL THOSE IN FAVOR OF ACCEPTING THE MINUTES AS READ, SAY "AYE"...THOSE OPPOSED, SAY "NAY"...THE MINUTES HAVE BEEN APPROVED AS SUBMITTED. THE PRESIDENT NOW ASKS IF THERE IS ANY OLD BUSINESS...THE PRESIDENT RECOGNIZES THELMA JANSON.

THANK YOU, PRESIDENT JANSON. I MOVE THAT WE CONTINUE OUR DISCUSSION OF WHY SO FEW PEOPLE WILL COME TO P.T.A. MEETINGS.

A MOTION HAS BEEN MADE TO CONTINUE OUR DISCUSSION OF WHY SO FEW PEOPLE COME TO P.T.A. MEETINGS. ALL THOSE IN FAVOR SAY, "AYE"...

THE PLACE WHERE STORE OWNERS
BUY SHOPPING CARTS

THE DANGERS OF RUNNING AROUND WITH THE WRONG CROWD

19

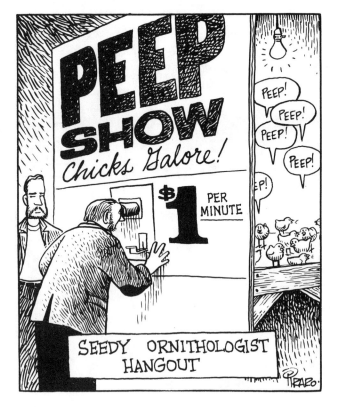

I CAN'T BAR YOU FROM THE FLIGHT BECAUSE OF THE WAY YOU'RE DRESSED, BUT MANY OF THE OTHER PASSENGERS ARE REFUSING TO GET ON— INCLUDING THE PILOT.

I'M SORRY, SIR, BUT THE LIMIT IS *ONE* LIFETIME SUPPLY OF THE *GUARANTEED FOR LIFE STAINLESS STEEL COMBS°* PER CUSTOMER.

24

29

31

33

36

37

NewsBulletin — Shortly before midnight last night, Calvin & Hobbes creator Bill Watterson finally agreed to a compromise over his much-lamented retirement, and will allow Billy, from Family Circus, to continue his strip.

Grown-ups are yucky!

yeah!

Billy (7)

PIRARO.

OKAY!! — EVERYBODY LINE UP FOR A FAMILY PHOTO, EXCEPT THOSE WHOSE LIFESTYLE THE REST OF US DON'T APPROVE OF!

HONESTY & HOLIDAYS DON'T MIX

PIRARO.

EX-HEAVYWEIGHT CHAMPION *SMOKIN' JOE FRAZIER* SUDDENLY FINDS HE IS BANNED FROM MOST PUBLIC BUILDINGS.

46

50

51

POPULAR BIRD TATTOO

CANNIBALS WAITING FOR THIS WEEK'S ISSUE OF *PEOPLE MAGAZINE*

64

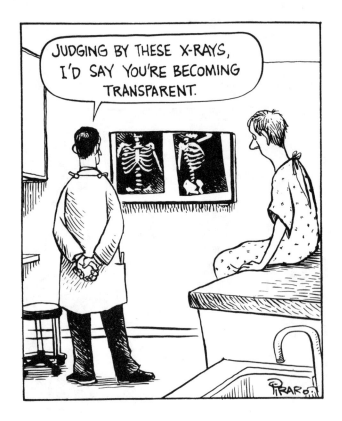

ANOTHER ALL-BUT-UNNOTICED FURNITURE UPRISING

70

71

72

80

YOUR HONOR, MY CLIENT HAS *NOT* SKIPPED TOWN —— IN THE PROCESS OF TAKING A *SAMPLE* OF HIS DNA, THE LAB TECHNICIAN INADVERTENTLY TOOK ALMOST *ALL* OF IT, LEAVING NOTHING BUT THIS SMALL PLATE OF GOO.

...PUT YOUR LEFT FOOT IN, TAKE YOUR LEFT FOOT OUT. PUT YOUR LEFT FOOT IN AND SHAKE IT ALL ABOUT...

HOKEY POKEY STEW

86

91

94

96

WE'RE NOT LEAVING THIS SPOT UNTIL I FIND OUT WHO STOLE MERIWETHER'S HAT FROM HIS LOCKER AND REPLACED IT WITH A LIVE BADGER!

DOZENS OF RUSH-HOUR MOTORISTS WERE TREATED FOR SHOCK TODAY WHEN A TRUCK CARRYING 400 CASES OF KETCHUP COLLIDED WITH A SHIPMENT OF MAN-NEQUINS, SPILLING THE CONTENTS OF BOTH ONTO THE EXPRESSWAY...

99

111